Lizzie Borden

Unlocked!

Ed Sams

Published by Yellow Tulip Press
P.O. Box 211
Ben Lomond, CA 95005
USA

Some photos from the collection of the Fall River Historical Society. Used with permission.

Fourth Edition
Printed in the United States of America

FOR SALLY

CONTENTS

CHAPTER 1
THE LIZZIE LEGEND

Lizzie Borden took an axe,
Gave her mother forty whacks;
When she saw what she had done,
She gave her father forty-one!

Everyone knows the ditty--sung to the tune of "Ta-Ra-Ra-Boom-De-Ay!"--but no one really knows the person behind the song. For more than one hundred years, Lizzie Borden and her hatchet have caused more confusion, speculation and debate than any other murder case in American history.

Who was Lizzie Borden and why should we care so? The American wit Dorothy Parker once wrote, "I will believe till eternity, or possibly beyond it, that Lizzie Borden did it with her little hatchet, and whoever says she didn't commits the sin of sins, the violation of an idol (Reach, 59)." Heady praise from one American original to another--but an idol?

Lizzie Borden, the acquitted suspect but legendary perpetrator of the grisly double murder of her father and stepmother, becomes in time all things to all people. In the more than one hundred years since the Fall River Murders, Lizzie has become the subject of plays, movies, an opera and a ballet. During her own time she was a *cause celebre* of a women's movement and an example of Christian piety. Her acquittal is a tribute to the American justice system and its main tenet of innocent until proven guilty. In many ways she is a success story, and it is how her own dark dreams coincide with the America Dream that makes her legendary.

Opinion about Lizzie was divided, even by those who knew her. During her trial, her able defense attorney George Robinson referred to her as "little girl," although she was a stout spinster of 32. No doubt the 12 good men and true on the jury saw her as a defenseless orphan, even if contrived by her own ingenuity. The neighborly Dr. Bowen, who was so helpful to Lizzie during the police investigation, no doubt felt some paternal concern over her, particularly considering the cryptic remark he made when he was caught burning evidence. Lizzie's sister Emma regarded herself as Lizzie's mother after their real mother died, even giving Lizzie her own bedroom after Lizzie's grand tour of Europe.

1

Whatever Lizzie's stepmother Abby thought, she kept to herself--even when Lizzie killed her cat, or complained of her to tradespeople, or refused to speak or eat meals with her. Certainly Bridget, the maid, thought well of Lizzie; she testified in court that she took Lizzie's side in family arguments. Lizzie was grateful enough for Bridget's testimony to buy Bridget a farm in Ireland--so long as she would never return to Fall River again.

Finally, the question is, what did Mr. Borden think of Lizzie? It would be natural for him to think of his youngest daughter as his "little girl" and treat her as the baby, but was there something else to their relationship? When his mutilated corpse was found, Lizzie's graduation ring was still worn around his little finger. This happened several months after he beheaded all of Lizzie's pigeons in their barn--the same barn in which Lizzie supposedly ate pears while his murder took place. Whatever Lizzie Borden was to all these people, she remains a cipher, the empty center to perhaps the most perplexing crime in American history.

■ ■ ■

CHAPTER 2

THE FALL RIVER MURDERS

What makes the Fall River murders so perplexing is that the motive, the weapon and the opportunity for such a crime are all seemingly absent. So is any exhibit of hard circumstantial evidence, although the case swims in a plethora of clues, secrets and mysteries. According to crime scholar Edmund Pearson, "the public's fascination with the case may have resulted from its very 'purity.' The murders, and Lizzie's guilt or innocence, were uncomplicated by such sins as ambition, robbery, greed, lust or other usual homicidal motives (Sifakis, 91)."

When the Fall River constabulary investigated the murders, they found no money or jewelry missing, not even small amounts of change or the packet of bus tickets as were taken in the daytime break-in at the Borden home 12 months earlier. Later, Prosecuting Attorney Knowlton hired a machinist who spent two days cracking open Andrew Borden's phenomenal safe in hopes of finding a missing will disinheriting both daughters. But Borden died intestate, leaving Lizzie and Emma to inherit his entire fortune.

Besides the lack of a clear motive for the murders, there was also the disconcerting lack of opportunity. Fall River found the entire Borden house locked up as usual, and during the two-and-a-half-hour period in which both murders were completed, the maid Bridget was outside the house washing windows and daughter Lizzie was inside the house reading a magazine. Even if one of the two committed the crime, the violent and bloody act should have been noisy enough to attract the attention of the other. And even if both were involved for some reason in this heinous enterprise, what became of the blood so conspicuously missing from the bludgeoned corpses of Mr. and Mrs. Borden?

Borden House Circa 1892

Perhaps most astonishing of all is the lack of a weapon. Every child jumping rope knows that "Lizzie Borden took an axe," yet as James Reach points out, the prosecution never proved the weapon was an axe (59). In fact, the prosecution tried its hardest to make a case for a handle-less hatchet smeared with ash that was found in the Borden basement. Yet microscopic examination of the blade revealed no traces of blood (Sullivan, 127). Evan Hunter believed Mrs. Borden was struck with a "heavy, sharp-edged candlestick," yet no axe, hatchet, or even candlestick could be found to substantiate these theories in a court of law.

The contrarieties of this case caused more than 1,900 divorces (according to a *New York Times* poll at the time) in which husbands and wives, arguing over Lizzie's guilt or innocence, de-cided that they were mutually incompatible (Sifakis, 91). Finally, one pamphlet was pub-lished in which the author threw up his hands and declared that with all the clues leading to dead ends, no one committed the murders (Radin, 267)!

Fall River Historical Society

The Murder Weapon?

In order to understand the compelling drama of the Borden saga, we must return to the scene of the crime during the sti-fling hot Thursday morning of a week-long heat wave--which culminated in two senseless murders.

■   ■   ■

CHAPTER 3

THE BORDENS OF FALL RIVER

The Borden family of Fall River, Massachusetts, were prominent citizens--not only because of Old Andrew Borden's wealth, but also because of their old New England name. Lizzie was ninth-generation on her father's side to live in Fall River, and she took her rightful place in Fall River society despite her father's miserly habits.

Old Andrew grew up poor and made his own wealth in his own way. According to one Fall River legend, "When he was an undertaker, he cut the feet off the corpses so that he could cram them into undersized coffins that he got cheap (Lincoln, 35)." Even after enjoying prosperity as a banker and slumlord, Andrew Borden did not mind selling eggs from his farm on Main Street. Perhaps this humble entrepreneurialism embarrassed Lizzie on her errands of mercy for the Christian Endeavor Society, the Fruit and Flower Mission and the Hospital of the Good Samaritan--but it hardly seems a motive for murder. Andrew Borden himself was not much of a church-goer or a socialite; his community activities were reserved for the many boards of directors to which he belonged. These positions of prestige and power included being president of Union Savings Bank, director of First National Bank, director of Durfee Safe Deposit & Trust Company, director of Globe Yarn Mill Company, director of Troy Cotton & Woolen Manufacturing Company and director of Merchants Manufacturing Company.

Andrew Borden

In spite of Andrew Borden's business drive and Lizzie Borden's social ambition, the Bordens lived quite modestly in a narrow little house on Second Street, a busy thoroughfare in the south part of town, heavily traveled in sight and sound of factories and ironworks and only a few hundred yards

The Borden Building in Fall River

from City Hall (Sullivan, 10). Despite the crowded neighborhood and proximity to the police station, none of the neighbors saw anything helpful the morning of the murders and the police that day were all off on a clambake at Rocky Point, Rhode Island (Sullivan, 31).

Thursday, August 4, 1892, began inauspiciously enough with leftovers for breakfast. At the wealthy Borden table on that hot summer morning, breakfast was a meal of johnny cakes, bread, coffee, cookies, week-old mutton and mutton soup. There was later to be some controversy over bananas: A visiting uncle, John Morse, recalled them at the table (Radin, 58); the maid, Bridget, disagreed, saying to the best of her belief, no bananas were served (Pearson, 197).

John Morse

The question of the morning meal proved to be an important one, for no less than two members of the Borden household had claimed only the day before that they were being poisoned. Mrs. Borden had gone to Dr. Bowen across the street with stories of an anonymous note claiming they were being poisoned (Lincoln, 62); later that evening, Lizzie told her friend Alice Russell, "Sometimes I think our milk might be poisoned (Sullivan, 98)."

The entire household had been sick for several days, some claim due to eating "warmed-over fish" before assaying the mutton (Lincoln, 61). The entire household at this time included Mr. and Mrs. Borden; Lizzie; and the maid, Bridget. Lizzie's older sister, Emma, was away visiting friends in Fairhaven. The unexpected guest, Uncle John Morse, who arrived without luggage the night before the murders, presumably knew enough to stick to bananas.

That fateful morning the elder Bordens had recovered enough to come downstairs and attempt the joint of mutton once more. Lizzie stayed upstairs, as was her habit, until the others had finished, so she could slip down unobserved and forage for herself. Andrew Borden was the first out the door to make business calls, followed shortly after by Uncle John gone a-visiting a distant niece who lived in town. Abby Borden, an overweight recluse, never left the house for business or social calls, but instead went

Abby Borden

to hide upstairs in the guest room, turkey duster in hand. Before she left the kitchen, Abby gave the curious order to Bridget to wash the windows. Washing windows in a heat wave must have been trying for the nauseated maid. Furthermore, the lowered windows must have made the air close inside the shut-up house for Abby and Lizzie, two women who hated and feared each other.

■ ■ ■

CHAPTER 4
THE FAMILY FEUD

Abby Durfee Gray wed Andrew Borden in 1864 when Lizzie was only two years old. For 30 years the two women lived together under one roof, yet on the day of Abby's murder Lizzie gave no indication that they ever got along. During the murder trial, Deputy Marshal John Fleet testified that on the day Abby died he asked Lizzie, "if she had any idea who could have killed her father and mother. Lizzie said, 'She's not my mother, Sir. She is my stepmother. My mother died when I was a child (Sullivan, 105).'" During the inquest, Lizzie commented:

> *I did not regard her as my mother, though she came there when I was young. I decline to say whether my relations between her and myself were those of mother and daughter or not. I called her Mrs. Borden and sometimes Mother. I stopped calling her Mother after the affair regarding her sister-in-law* (Sullivan, 213).

The affair with Abby's sister-in-law concerns one of Andrew Borden's lonesome acts of generosity. Abby's family, the Durfees, were not as well off as the Bordens. In fact, their only property was a double dwelling owned by Abby's mother, which also housed Abby's sister-in-law and family. According to Victoria Lincoln, Abby's mother, Mrs. Gray, put her two-dwelling house up for sale. Andrew bought half in his wife's name, allowing Abby's sister to stay in one-half of the house. Andrew had old Ferry Street Cottage made over into a double dwelling and deeded it over to his daughters. Each half-dwelling cost $1,500 (40-41).

One would think such fair and even-handed treatment would be rewarded, or at least go unpunished. But the two unmarried daughters took umbrage over their father's interest in their stepmother's family. As Lizzie put it at the inquest, "We thought what he did to her people he ought to do for his own (Sullivan, 217)." Unfortunately, when he did for his own by deeding Emma and Lizzie their grandfather's house on Ferry Street (Lincoln, 41), the upkeep of the rental property proved to be burdensome for the ladies, so Andrew bought it back a few weeks before his murder (Sullivan, 22).

It is difficult to say if the death of Mrs. Borden's cat occurred before or during this feud. It in itself would be cause enough for Mrs. Borden to fear her stepdaughter. Borden scholars Pearson and Radin both allude to the rumors of Lizzie's cruelty to animals despite the evidence of her will's munificent bequest to the Fall River Animal Rescue Society. Robert Sullivan, in his objective research of the case, *Good-bye Lizzie Borden*, actually interviewed Mrs. Abby Whitehead Potter (Abby Borden's niece and namesake), who remembered her aunt and this chilling tale:

> *Lizzie Borden had company and my aunt had a tabby cat and the cat was trained so that it would touch the latch--you know, it was [sic] latches in those days--she'd touch the latch and the door would open. So the cat went in where Lizzie was entertaining and she took it out and shut the door again, and came back so this is what she told Aunt Abby and Abby told my mother; Lizzie Borden finally excused herself and went downstairs--took the cat downstairs--and put the carcass on the chopping block and chopped its head off. My aunt for days wondered where that cat was--all she talked about. Finally, Lizzie said, 'You go downstairs and you'll find your cat.' My aunt did* (Sullivan, 23).

■ ■ ■

CHAPTER 5

GRUESOME DEATHS

Whether the story is accurate or not, by 9 o'clock that hot August morning Abby had died much the same way as the cat. Her head was nearly torn off her shoulders by a blunt instrument as she lay face down on the floor of the upstairs bedroom. Forensic experts at the time judge that she had seen her attacker when struck (Radin, 147). When she was examined by Dr. Bowen, he found her head crushed by 19 axe or hatchet wounds in the back of the scalp (Sullivan, 31). One wound at the back of the neck was misdirected, for the blow had cut a "great and grotesque flap" from the back of the scalp (Sullivan, 31). Because of the lack of blood, it has been surmised that Abby died from the first blow, and with death her heart stopped pumping blood. As Lincoln writes:

> Abby had apparently been hacked by someone who stood
> astride the body after the first blow (probably the one on the
> nape of the neck) had felled her. Her blood had spurted for-
> ward and not high or wide; there was none on the bedspread
> just beside her, and of the wall in front of her head only the
> skirting board was stained (114).

Once the killer finished with the victim, the 200-pound corpse lay sprawled out on the knees face down waiting to be discovered two hours later.

Meanwhile, Old Andrew Borden went calmly on his rounds of business to the Union Savings Bank, to the National Union Bank, to the First National Bank of Fall River and then to see one of his tenants, the hatter Jonathan Clegg. At the haberdasher's shop, Borden was seen picking up a discarded lock, "badly bro-ken," and slipping it into his pocket (Sullivan, 27). At 10:40 a.m. his next-door neighbor, Mrs. Kelly, saw him at his front door as she hurried on to a dentist's appointment. He would not leave the house alive, for less than an hour later his daughter Lizzie called up to the maid, resting in her attic room, "Come down quick! Father's dead! Somebody came in and killed him (Pearson, 201)!"

Friendly Dr. Bowen, who lived across the street, was summoned at once. Later, when recalling the sight of the dead body in the cramped little sitting room, he said, "Physician that I am, and accustomed to all kinds of horrible sights, it sickened me to look upon the dead man's face (Pearson, 230)."

Here is Edmund Pearson's famous description of the scene:

> *This was a small room, nearly square, with but two windows, both on the south side. The floor was covered with the usual garish, flowered carpet, customary in such houses at that time, and the wall paper was of a similarly disturbing pattern. The furniture was mahogany or black walnut, upholstered with the invariable black horsehair. On the north side of the room, opposite the windows, was a large sofa, and on this lay the dead body of Mr. Borden with his head and face so hacked as to be unrecognizable even to his friend and physician, Dr. Bowen* (Sullivan, 203).

Again, the mysterious murderer struck violently to the head. According to Robert Sullivan:

> *Borden's head was bent slightly to the right, but his face was almost unrecognizable as human; one eye had been cut in half and protruded in a ghastly manner, his nose had been severed, and there were eleven distinct cuts within a relatively small area extending from the eye and nose to the ears. Fresh blood was still seeping from the wounds, which were so severe that the first of the eleven blows must have killed him* (30).

■ ■ ■

CHAPTER 6

THE MISSING BLOOD

One of the greatest sources of speculation in the Fall River Murders was the lack of blood. In both cases, the heads of the victims had been nearly ripped from their shoulders, yet neither the upstairs guest room nor the downstairs sitting room showed more than traces of blood. "There were blood spots on the floor, on the wall over the sofa, on a picture hanging on the wall, but, Bowen said, there was 'nothing to indicate the slaughter that had taken place. The clothing on the body was not at all disturbed, nor was there any injury other than to the face (Sullivan, 30).'"

The absence of blood on Lizzie Borden's person so soon after the murders weighed heavily in her favor during the investigation. Adelaide Churchill, the neighbor who stayed with Lizzie until the doctor arrived, testified in court that she did not see any blood on Lizzie's dress when she left at noon. According to Mrs. Churchill, "I stood in front of her, rubbing both her hands and fanning her, and I did not see any blood on her hands or on her face, nor any disarrangement of her hair (Sullivan, 95)." Such a spotless appearance seems impossible if Lizzie indeed committed the crime, for she had at best 20 minutes after her father fell asleep to strike him 11 times about the head, hide the murder weapon and clean all evidence off her clothes and body.

Neighbor Adelaide Churchill

Robert Sullivan suggests that the floor plan of the sitting room provides the solution to the puzzle. According to Sullivan, the horsehair couch upon which Andrew Borden lay for his nap was flush with the door leading into the dining room. With his head resting upon the arm of the couch nearest the dining room, Old Andrew was in striking distance of anyone behind the dining room door. In fact, there was a version of the Lizzie Borden song current at the time of the trial that suggested this modus operandi:

> *Lizzie Borden took an axe*
> *And gave her mother 40 whacks.*
> *Then she stood behind the door*
> *And gave her father 40 more*
> (Sullivan, 182-183)

Appealing though this jingle may be, hitting a target while behind a door takes delicate precision. Andrew's death was not delicate. Another theory of how Lizzie managed not to be caught red-handed centers around her father's Prince Albert coat. Andrew Borden always wore this garment on business calls, then habitually removed and hung it on the hat rack before taking a nap. However, when Andrew Borden was discovered, this prized possession was found rolled over the sofa arm stained with the victim's blood. Victoria Lincoln believes that Lizzie "saw the Prince Albert on the hat rack, reached out and, sheltered out of sight of the door, slipped it on back to front like a huge butcher's apron (Lincoln, 135)," and did the deed so celebrated in verse and song.

Nevertheless, for sheer horrific appeal, the most popular theory of how Lizzie committed the murders was in the nude. By undressing before each crime and sponging down afterwards, Lizzie could get away with murder without any signs giving her away. Reach alludes to this rumor in his article (61). Sifakis mentions it in his *Encyclopedia of American Crime,* but with this proviso: "There was a theory that Lizzie had stripped naked to do the deeds and then had put her clothes back on, but that certainly would have involved a great

Andrew Borden's Mutilated Corpse

risk of her being seen by the maid (90)." One doubts the risk of being seen killing someone while in the nude is any greater than the risk of being seen while fully clothed. Strangely, this bare-bones theory was originally put forth by Lizzie's own attorney who suggested at the trial, "I would not wonder if they are not going to claim that this woman denuded herself and did not have any dress on at all when she committed either murder (Lincoln, 281)."

14

Whether Lizzie committed the crimes or not, her hands being unsoiled with her parents' blood leaves open an intriguing question. As one student of the Borden case suggested, there's something suspicious about a daughter finding her father murdered and *not* having any blood on her (Pearson, 240).

■ ■ ■

Fall River Historical Society

Abby Borden's Corpse,
Discovered in the Guest Room

The Borden Guest Room

CHAPTER 7

THE MIND OF LIZZIE BORDEN

Consider now the mind of Lizzie Borden. At this point, when the bodies are discovered, the unchronicled lives of the Bordens become history and Lizzie begins to speak for herself. If, in fact, she was neck-deep in patricide, what was she thinking of? From her coolly civil responses to questions from the authorities, to the dream-like stream of consciousness in her inquest testimony, Lizzie reveals the weather of her mind in her selection of bizarre details that made up, for her, the day her parents died. The pears, the locks, the sick note from an anonymous friend, the handleless hatchet, the poison, the vermin, the burned dress--all paint an absorbing picture of the person who was Lizzie Borden. It is like looking through a clear keyhole into a dark room. Victoria Lincoln describes Lizzie's transparent opaqueness as "this tic, combined with her compulsion to mention and explain away incriminating details. It is strange to study the mind of one who is at once so unimaginative and so wholly out of touch with reality (Lincoln, 172)."

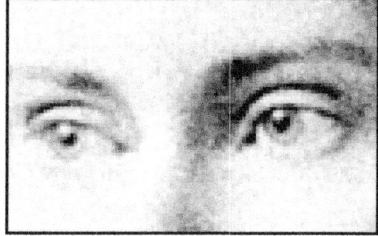

As a little girl, Victoria Lincoln knew Lizzie Borden at a time long after the trial when Lizzie and Emma moved to Maplecroft, a house on the hill in the good part of town. From her own observation and interviews with Fall River residents, Lincoln reports "hearsay evidence" of Lizzie's "spells" leading her to this conjecture. Lizzie Borden suffered from psychomotor epilepsy, a strange seizure of the temporal lobe that occurred during her menstrual cycle (46). The petit mal seizure of psychomotor epilepsy has one distinct symptom: a brown-out in which patients carry out their actions in a dream state, aware of every action without knowing what they are doing (43). Such a very appealing hypothesis is perhaps a little too elaborate. Temporary--or even permanent--insanity is all too believable without it being diagnosed as epilepsy.

Nevertheless, Lincoln's description of Lizzie's movements as "sleepwalking" is consistent with Lizzie's own words. She confided in her friend Alice Russell the night before the murders, "I feel as if I wanted

17

to sleep with my eyes half open--with one eye open half the time--for fear they will burn the house down over us (Sullivan, 99)," and "I am afraid somebody will do something. I don't know but what somebody will do something (99)."

When Alice Russell asked what, Lizzie said, "Well, I don't know. I feel depressed. I feel as if something was hanging over me at times, no matter where I am. When I was at Marion, the girls were laughing and talking and having a good time, and this feeling came over me, and one of them spoke and said, 'Lizzie, why don't you talk?' I don't know what was said after that (Sullivan, 97)." Lizzie Borden seemed only partially aware of the turmoil boiling inside her.

Certainly the mind of Lizzie Borden seemed to hold two entirely different personalities. While one kept awake with one eye open, the other, deep inside her, slept. Her dual nature becomes apparent in the testimony her kinsman, Hiram Harrington, gave to the police. There is Lizzie, the good daughter, who told Harrington on the day of the murders that she helped her father:

> ...to get a comfortable reclining position on the lounge, and asked
> him if he did not wish the blinds closed to keep out the sun, so he
> could have a nice nap. She pressed him to allow her to place an
> afghan over him, but he said he did not need it. Then she asked him
> tenderly several times if he was perfectly comfortable, if there was
> anything she could do for him, and upon receiving assurance to the
> negative she withdrew (Brown, 104-105).

Andrew Borden would never rise from the bed his daughter so carefully made for him.

On the other hand, there was Lizzie, the bad daughter, of whom Harrington said:

> Lizzie is of a repellent disposition, and after an unsuccessful
> passage with her father would become sulky and refuse to speak
> to him for days at a time. She moved in the best society in Fall
> River, was a member of the Congregational Church, and is a
> brilliant conversationalist. She thought she ought to entertain
> as others did, and felt with her father's wealth, she was

expected to hold her end up with others of her set. Her fa-
ther's constant refusal to allow her to entertain lavishly an-
gered her. I have heard many bitter things she has said of her
father, and know she was deeply resentful of her father's
maintained stand in this matter (Brown, 106-107).

Perhaps the paradox of having the reality of wealth but the appearance
of poverty drove Lizzie to develop two personalities to cope with this
contradiction. Simultaneously, she appears the modest church-going
spinster and the willful, extravagant heiress. A strong-willed, covetous
nature masked as virtue was all part of the Borden legacy. In a letter to
the Fall River *Daily Globe*, August 17, 1892, an anonymous Borden rela-
tive expounded this family characteristic:

By blood! If she did it, the old Borden nerve, grit, and cheek
are not degenerated. No woman except a Borden could have
done it, and yet it seems impossible that a woman could do it.
I have watched her indomitable nerve and bearing with admi-
ration, and I recalled that Aunt Nannie Borden, who ran out
when the bullets were flying, and kicked a wounded British
redcoat and then tore up her skirts for wadding; and I

Lizzie (front row right) and the Ladies of the Congregational Church

> *remember that my poor old grandmother when a constable*
> *seized her broadcloth cloak for grandfather's rum bill, when*
> *he read his warrant and said: 'I seize this cloak,' she took him*
> *by the throat and said: 'God! And I seize you!' And he was*
> *glad to drop the cloak and git. So if this girl has done this*
> *thing it is the old Borden nerve and grit that carried her*
> *through, and I predict that she will not wilt. No, by blood*
> (Brown, 15)*!*

This strange combination of scruples and ruthlessness seemed to be known and accepted by all of Fall River. Lizzie's own friends remarked that it was highly unlikely Lizzie would kill anybody, "but it would be absolutely impossible for her to lie about it (Brown, 115)."

Even still, in adversity there was always something very shrewd and determined about Lizzie Borden. By noon on the day of the murders, Lizzie, Bridget, Dr. Bowen, Mrs. Churchill and Lizzie's friend, Miss Alice Russell, were alone in the Borden home. The police had not arrived. The body of Mrs. Borden had not yet been discovered; indeed, no one knew where she was. Lizzie said she had received a note from a sick friend; then later she thought she heard Mrs. Borden upstairs. She repeatedly tried to get someone to go upstairs to Mrs. Borden while Dr. Bowen was examining her father. Finally, Bowen was done and called for a sheet to cover the body. "Better get two," Lizzie added (Radin, 265).

Another example of Lizzie's penchant for dry understatement was provided by Police Matron Hannah Reagan. During Lizzie's stay in Fall River Jail, Hannah bet Lizzie a dollar that Lizzie could not crack an egg on its side. Lizzie reduced the bet to a quarter, tried and failed, causing her to observe, "That is the first thing that I undertook that I never could (Sullivan, 140)." An intriguing remark considering the cracked condition of the victims' skulls.

Victoria Lincoln writes of Lizzie and Emma's visit to a friend:

> *Now at one end of the grounds was an old woodshed very di-*
> *lapidated, which spoiled the view of the bay. Lizzie's hostess*
> *looking at it said to Emma, 'The very next time Mike comes,*
> *we must remember to have him knock that thing down for*

firewood. 'Why wait for Mike?' she [Lizzie] cried. 'Give me the axe (Lincoln, 303)*!'*

Dr. Seabury Bowen

Lizzie never grasped the appropriate. When the police finally arrived after the murders, Lizzie acted more like a concerned citizen than a daughter in shock. Much was made of her disinterest. Adelaide Churchill, who had gone up for the sheets and found Abby, swore, "I never saw Lizzie in tears that morning at any time (Sullivan, 95)." Bridget swore that she never said Lizzie was crying at any time (Sullivan, 92). Captain Harrington declared, "She was not in tears at any part of the interview. Her voice was at all times steady (Sullivan, 111)." One can almost hear the tongues of Fall River wagging. Even in New York, sensibilities were shocked. The *Times*, almost grumblingly, reported, "The fact that so little ado was made by those who were most directly interested, and so little attempt was made at first to discover the possible murderer, is strengthening the police in the opinions they now hold (*New York Times*, August 5, 1892: 2)."

Fall River Historical Society

Bridget Sullivan

To do the police justice, they had eliminated many suspects before considering the unthinkable. It was inevitable that Lizzie would become the prime suspect, especially after they learned she had tried to buy poison the week before. Still, legion are the false trails the Fall River police followed before returning to the scene of the crime.

■ ■ ■

CHAPTER 8
THE INVESTIGATION

T he Fall River Police were subject to much criticism for their initial handling of the murder case. Though most of the force were off on an unofficial holiday in Rhode Island, there were officers still on duty. Unfortunately, they were short-handed and unprepared for such an admittedly abnormal crime. The apocryphal story recounted by Edmund Pearson in *The Trial of Lizzie Borden* underscores the shock and confusion that resulted that day when Officer George Allen was on duty. He writes:

> An unofficial but reliable account of Allen's visits, received
> from two newspaper reporters, says that the sight of Mr. Borden's body nearly scared the officer 'out of his wits.' He ran
> back to the station, and to his chief gasped out: 'He's dead!'
> The unperturbed marshal replied: 'Who's dead, you fool?'
> Allen managed to say: 'Old Mr. Borden!' The marshal could
> not leave his post, but ordered Allen back to the house of
> death. In ten minutes, however, Officer Allen came panting back again, this time croaking, 'She's dead (165)!'

In a small town where citizens slept on hot summer nights with their front doors open, and everyone knew everybody, such a crime was unthinkable. The immediate assumption was that the murderer must be an outsider. Therefore, one of the earliest theories supposed that the murderer was concealed about the house when Mr. Borden came in (*New York Times*, August 5, 1892: 1)." Certainly the neighbors recalled seeing an odd assortment of strangers on Second Street that day. A Dr. Handy reported a "wild-eyed man." Several saw a "Portuguese," and several others noticed a buggy with two passengers make a U-turn in the street that morning. Here is the front-page story in the *New York Times* from August 7, 1892:

> A horse and buggy turned into Second Street out of Spring,
> and stopped in front of the Borden residence. A man who is
> employed nearby sat in his buggy almost opposite and facing
> south. He had ample opportunity and time to take a careful
> look at the vehicle, and the circumstance of the two strange
> men calling at the Borden house made an impression on

his mind which he remembers distinctly. One of the men got out of the buggy and rang the doorbell. As he stood there the observer saw him plainly, and remembers that his description was that of a man about twenty-five years of age, with sallow complexion, soft hat, dark trousers, with a wide strop [sic] of dark material down the leg and russet, or baseball shoes. He was 5 feet 9 inches high. Mr. Borden opened the door and the man was admitted. The man who entered remained about ten minutes and then came out with his hat in his hand. The police assiduously tracked down the whereabouts of all these suspicious characters: the stranger in the buggy turned out to be a lost tourist who missed his train connection, the Portuguese was a Swede, and Dr. Handy's "wild-eyed" man was a tramp called Mike the Soldier who suffered from DTs (Pearson, 219-220).

Edwin Porter, in his suppressed book, *The Fall River Tragedy*, explains how difficult it would be to hide inside the Borden house:

He had to deal with a family of six persons in an unpretentious two-and-a-half story house, the rooms of which were all connected and in which it would have been a difficult matter to stifle sound. He must catch Mr. Borden alone and either asleep, or off his guard, and kill him with one fell blow. The faintest outcry would have sounded an alarm. He must also encounter Mrs. Borden alone and fell her, a heavy woman, noiselessly. To do this he must either make his way from the sitting room on the ground floor to the spare bedroom above the parlor and avoid five persons in the passage, or he must conceal himself in one of the rooms upstairs and make the descent under the same conditions. The murdered woman must not lisp a syllable at the first attack, and her fall must not attract attention. He must then conceal the dripping implement of death and depart in daylight by a much-frequented street (Pearson, 212).

Nevertheless, the police had it upon very good authority that a burglar was seen around the Borden place and a stranger was even heard threatening Mr. Borden. The person who heard and saw all these nefariious occurrences was Lizzie Borden. According to Michael Mullaly, a policeman on duty, Lizzie told him she saw a man around the house sometime before with dark clothes on. Dr. Bowen also confirmed the story: "She then said that she overheard loud conversation several times recently (Sullivan, 89-90)." Furthermore, Lizzie told Deputy Marshall Fleet that, "About two weeks ago a man came to the house to the front door, and had some talk with Father and talked as though he was angry. He was talking about a store, and father said to him, "I cannot let you the store for that purpose (Sullivan, 105)." She went on to say that, "About nine o'clock that morning a man came to the door and was talking with her father; she thought they were talking about a store, and he spoke like an Englishman (Lincoln, 120)." According to Lincoln, a resident of Fall River, "Englishman" means "Lancashire-man," or mill worker (120). Since there were several mills in Fall River and plenty of mill workers, this lead did not take the police very far.

A recent theory by Arnold Brown gives strange legitimacy to the dark stranger scenario. According to Brown in *Lizzie Borden: The Final Chapter*, "Andrew Borden had not fathered 'only two' children. In addition to a third daughter who was dead, he had, by a woman named Phebe Hath-

away, fathered an illegitimate son whose existence was whispered on The Hill and was more than common knowledge within the Borden clan (Brown, 116)." Brown says this William Borden, a demented apple farmer, called upon Andrew Borden one day to claim his birthright and ended up committing the crime for which his half-sister Lizzie was blamed. Brown's admirable research proves the existence of one William Borden and establishes his violent character, as well as arguing persuasively of William's illegitimate birth. But the only evidence linking William Borden to Andrew Borden is the opinion of

Deputy Marshall Fleet

Arnold Brown's next-door neighbor in Florida whose dead father-in-law knew William as a child and suspected him of the crime. Nevertheless, this new spin to the old yarn gives new significance to Lizzie's testimony: "There was a man that came there that he had trouble with, I don't know who the man was. The man had an interest in a Borden property. 'I would like to have that place,' he said. I heard Father order

25

him out (Brown, 117)." Even if William Borden was the murderer, Brown concedes that Lizzie must have known and was no doubt involved in arranging the visit, if not the hatchet job.

Likewise, the Fall River police, after checking the house and finding the front and screen doors, the basement door and most of the bedroom doors locked, were finally considering the possibility of the murders being an inside job. With this new direction, the suspicion fell upon the most likely suspect: Lizzie's Uncle John. John Vinculum Morse, brother of Lizzie's late mother Sarah Morse Borden, had chosen the wrong time for a surprise visit. The newspapers were quick to point the finger of blame at him (*New York Times*, Friday, August 5, 1892: 2). A crowd of angry Fall River citizens mobbed him the day after the murders, and much was made of his unexpected arrival the day before the murders without a valise. The police were looking for more than one man, for two had been seen in the strange buggy on Second Street. And it was common knowledge that Uncle John consorted with vagabond horse traders who were camped outside the city limits. The *New York Times* gives a very colorful description of these suspects:

> *In West Port, at the head of the river, there is a camp of itinerant horse traders who have been operating in that vicinity for three weeks or more. They go in and out of New Bedford continually and Morse has been seen to have to do with these people. Among them was a man who fills precisely the description of the one seen by the boy on Thursday noon, the young man on Monday morning, and the Frenchman on Thursday afternoon. This man appeared to be the principal of the traders, and was not to be conversed with about trifling matters or on subjects other than those pertaining to horse trading. He admitted being from the West, but refused to say what part of the West. His tribe have the characteristics of men leading a roving life not unlike that of Gypsies. They dress in coarse, heavy garments, and live in tents in the woods* (Sunday, August 7, 1892: 1).

Exciting though the possibility of an outlaw band might be, the police soon had to give up the horse traders and Uncle John as another false lead. Uncle John quickly provided the authorities with a plausible alibi (his niece could testify as to the time of his visit), and so the connection with the Gypsies camped outside of town disappeared. Mr. Morse also courted the press in order to press his case before the court.

The *New York Times* reports that:

> *Mr. Morse came from the house and talked freely with a*
> *group of reporters. He said it was a terrible thing to be sus-*
> *pected and shadowed as he had been but he courts the fullest*
> *investigation and is anxious and willing to do all that he can to trace*
> *the perpetrators of the great crime* (Sunday, August 7, 1892: 1).

No doubt the most exotic theory about mysterious strangers as murder suspects concerns escaped mutineers. A news report published in nearby Lynn, Massachusetts, on August 13, 1892, claimed the motive of the Borden murders was revenge. According to the article, Andrew and Abby Borden took a cruise several years earlier on the schooner *Jefferson Borden*. The men on board protested harsh treatment and tried to take over the ship. The mutiny was squelched, and Andrew Borden's testimony convicted the ring leaders--two Americans, two Englishmen and one Portuguese. Two of the nationalities of the mutineers fit the descriptions given of strangers heard and seen in Fall River that unfortunate morning. Even better, a union agitator named Sullivan had petitioned President Harrison to release these maritime felons from Thomaston Prison, and they were pardoned eight months before the murders. It was a great story that tied up a lot of loose ends--except Old Andrew had never left Fall River to go on a cruise and Abby never left the house. The story was discredited in the *New York Times* the day after the Lynn story (August 14, 1892: 8).

Public opinion was also against Bridget. Letters poured into the Fall River Police Station, urging that they arrest her and her confessor. "Beware of Jesuits!" one letter warned (Pearson, 239). Certainly Bridget had as much opportunity to commit the murders as Lizzie. However, there is the question of motive. If Bridget committed the crime, why?

Edward Radin suggests in his book, *Lizzie Borden: The Untold Story,* that Bridget did not need a reason. Radin claims domestics may commit crimes of violence without provocation. He writes, "In a murder case I covered as a reporter, a young bride was killed by a window washer because she ordered him to use ammonia in the water and he resented being told what to do (Radin, 230)."

Victoria Lincoln also considers the possibility of Bridget being implicated, hedging her bets: "Lizzie committed the murders, or Bridget committed them with Lizzie's full knowledge and consent (45)." Lincoln offers no motive to entice the maid to mayhem.

Evan Hunter suggests a motive in his fictional *Lizzie:* "Mrs. Borden caught Lizzie in bed with Bridget and was bludgeoned with a heavy, sharp-edged candlestick. Andrew Borden was killed because he saw the candlestick and guessed the truth (Gates, 12)." There were rumors throughout Lizzie's life that she was a lesbian, but Bridget wed in Montana and had many children (Hunter, 406).

Emma Borden also came under suspicion. After all, she inherited, too. Emma is blamed for starting the daughters' feud with their stepmother. Even with her perfect alibi of visiting friends out of town, theorists have still implicated Emma at the scene of the crime. Sifakis writes: "She too lived under a cloud and there was even speculation that she was the killer. At the time of the murder Emma had been staying overnight with friends, but some insisted she could have returned home, committed the crimes and returned to her friends unseen (91)." Frank Spierling, who uncovered the Byzantine governmental plot behind the Jack the Ripper murders in England, goes one better by claiming Emma did it to avoid being disinherited (Gates, 12). Further-more, "Emma did rent a buggy which was reportedly seen outside the Borden house shortly before the murders (Nash, 440)." Though how Emma managed to slip back into town unnoticed, let alone into her own house, must be left to Spierling to explain.

Inevitably, the police began to look more closely at Lizzie Borden, especially after her attempts to buy poison became known.

■   ■   ■

Emma Borden

Side Entrance to the Borden House

CHAPTER 9
POISON!

Naturally, the Fall River constabulary were reluctant to accuse an heiress of one of the town's leading families, especially since there was no real evidence supporting such a conjecture. The strongest circumstantial evidence was known a week after the murders when Eli Bence, a druggist for King's pharmacy in Fall River, identified Lizzie Borden as a customer wanting prussic acid on Wednesday, the day before the murders.

Prussic acid is one of the most violent corrosives known, and Bence reasonably refused to sell even a dime's worth. The customer Bence identified as Lizzie claimed she wanted the poison to treat her sealskin cape for moths. Prussic acid would be absurd for such a purpose, for sealskin provides "no indus for insect eggs and is naturally immune to moths (Lincoln, 253)." However, this information, corroborated by two disinterested bystanders, was added to Dr. Bowen's reluctant testimony of Abby Borden's fears of being poisoned. Together, both stories established a predisposition on Lizzie's part to kill. All this came out at the inquest, in which Lizzie behaved in such a suspicious way as to suggest to many her guilt. The *New York Times* on Saturday, August 6, 1892, gives a picture of the proceedings:

> The demeanor of Miss Lizzie through the trying ordeal of
> being confronted with the man who says that she asked about
> poison was that of contempt and scorn. In fact, her conduct
> as observed by the police since the affair happened has been
> strange, inasmuch as she stood the pointed questioning of all
> who interviewed her with the show of no other feeling than
> that of a disinterested party (2).

By nightfall, Lizzie was arrested for the murders. Marshall Hilliard told her, "I have here a warrant for your arrest, for the murder of Andrew J. Borden. Do you wish it read?" Lizzie replied, "You need not read it (Sullivan, 45)." The *New York Times* wrote the following day, "The lady took the announcement of her arrest with surprising calmness (August 12, 1892: 2)."

Despite the obvious multiple blows with a blunt instrument, the deaths of Abby and Andrew Borden were suspected to be caused by poison up until the time of the trial in June of 1893. Theories that both had been drugged before the bludgeoning explained the absence of alarm or struggle from either victim. However, the rumors of poison were put to rest by three medical examiners.

Dr. William Dolan, who was on the scene the day of the murders, described to the court the care that was taken with the medical evidence:

> *'I left the Borden house and returned at three o'clock that af-
> ternoon when I conducted autopsies on both of the bodies on
> the dining room table. I removed the stomachs from both bod-
> ies, tying each at both ends and putting them into separate,
> clean jars which I sealed* (Sullivan, 121).'

Dr. Edward S. Wood, Professor of Chemistry at Harvard Medical School, testified to the contents of the stomachs:

> *'I first examined the stomach of Mrs. Andrew J. Borden. It
> was a normal stomach and its contents were, upon my exami-
> nation, found to be of a solid consistency: four-fifths solid
> food and one-fifth liquid. In the stomach contents I found par-
> tially digested starch: wheat found normally in bread or cake,
> slightly digested muscular fiber, meat, and an undigested
> skin of an apple. I next examined the stomach of Andrew J.
> Borden and found it to be a normal organ. The contents, how-
> ever, differed from those found in the stomach of Mrs. Bor-
> den; first, there was much more of contents, they consisted of
> nine-tenths liquid and one-tenth solid matter, only a few
> starch granules, a few muscle fibers from meat, and some
> vegetable tissue, the residue of a digested apple or pear* (Sulli-
> van, 125).'

The examination of the stomachs revealed no drugs or poisons. Furthermore, Frank W. Draper, M.D., examined the Bordens' intestines and found no evidence of drugs or poison either.

As for Lizzie's own concern about the milk, the *New York Times* "proved the milk drank by the Borden family was not poisoned when it was taken from the Borden farm and brought to the city. Members of the family in charge of the farm drank it, and they were affected in no no-ticeable way (August 12, 1892: 2)."

■   ■   ■

Newspaper Artist's Rendering of Lizzie's Trial

CHAPTER 10
THE TRIALS OF LIZZIE BORDEN

Lizzie Borden was involved in four legal proceedings; in only one did she give direct testimony. That was during the inquest, and it was on the basis of that strange testimony, partly curt and partly digressive, that she was held over for a grand jury hearing, a preliminary hearing and, finally, the murder trial itself.

The inquest was held on August 10, 1892, six days after the murder. It was suspended by Judge Blaisdel the following day. Presumably, he had heard enough to have Lizzie arrested that night. Lizzie Borden's inquest testimony is important because it is the only legal record of her view of the facts that fateful morning of August 4. However, her view of the facts as an eye witness to the events of the day only added more confusion to the mystery. Her comments started out dryly enough. When Prosecuting Attorney Knowlton asked, "Were you always cordial with your stepmother?" Lizzie countered, "That depends upon one's idea of cordiality (Sullivan, 212-213)." When asked to elaborate, Lizzie embarked on a free-form stream of consciousness, making it difficult to follow her train of thought:

Knowlton

'I always went to my sister. She was older than I was. I don't know but that my father and stepmother were happily united. I never knew of any difficulty between them, and they seemed to be affectionate. The day they were killed I had on a blue dress. I changed it in the afternoon and put on a print dress. Mr. Morse came into our house whenever he wanted to. He has been here once since the river was frozen over. I don't know how often he came to spend the nights, because I had been away so much. I have not been away much during the year (Sullivan, 213).'

Such apparent contradictions continue in her account of her father's return from his morning rounds:

> *'I was in the kitchen reading when my father returned. I stayed in
> my room long enough to sew a piece of lace on a garment. That was
> before he came back. I don't know where Maggie [Lizzie's name
> for Bridget] was. I think she let my father in, and that he rang the
> bell. I understood Maggie to say he said he had forgotten his key. I
> think I was upstairs when my father came in, and I think I was on
> the stairs when he entered (213).'*

The district attorney asked Lizzie if she was in the kitchen reading or on
the stairs when her father returned. Lizzie's reply was, "You have asked
me so many questions, I don't know what I have said (214)." Perhaps
the most intriguing piece of Lizzie's testimony was her barn alibi, which
accounted for her whereabouts during the 20-minute span in which her
father was being murdered:

> *'When I went out to the barn I left him on the sofa. The last thing I
> said was to ask him if he wanted the window left that way. Then I
> went to the barn to get some lead for a sinker. I went upstairs in the
> barn. There was a bench there which contained some lead. I un-
> hooked the screen door when I went out. I don't know when Bridget
> got through washing the windows inside. I knew she washed the
> windows outside. I knew she didn't wash the kitchen windows, but I
> didn't know whether she washed the sitting room windows or not. I
> thought the flats [flatirons] would be hot by the time I got back. I
> had no fishing apparatus, but there was some at the farm. It is five
> years since I used the fish line. I don't think there were any fish lines
> suitable for use at the farm (Sullivan, 214-215).'*

Here, District Attorney Knowlton interrupted Lizzie: "What! Did you think
you would find sinkers in the barn (215)?" Lizzie replied in the affirmative.
Her father had told her that there "was lead and nails in the barn." Knowlton
asked, "Did you do nothing besides look for sinkers in the twenty minutes?"
Lizzie answered, "Yes, sir, I ate some pears." He asked, "Would it take you all
that time to eat a few pears?" Calmly, Lizzie replied, "I do not do things in a
hurry (215)."

Unless the Bordens had been killed by two different murderers, coincidentally
using similar murder weapons on the same day, the real murderer would not

have hurried. There would have been time after Abby Borden was killed around 9 a.m. for the killer to sit down and read a magazine or perhaps eat pears until Andrew Borden came home and was killed at 11:30.

Evidently, Judge Blaisdel heard enough to suspend the inquest and immediately begin a preliminary hearing. Lizzie was arrested the evening of the suspended inquest, Thursday, August 11, and arraigned the following morning. The purpose of the preliminary hearing was to determine "probable cause." All Judge Blaisdel needed to hear was enough circumstantial evidence to warrant having the accused stand trial. The inquest testimony of Dr. Bowen and Mr. Bence concerning poison, as well as Lizzie's own ominous accounts, had already persuaded the judge that Lizzie was the prime suspect. Therefore, the preliminary hearing was a mere formality. In fact, Judge Blaisdel suspended the inquest where he was presiding in order to preside over the arraignment that held Lizzie Borden without bail in Taunton Jail until her trial 10 months later. Although Judge Blaisdel was well within his rights to officiate at both legal proceedings, some have questioned the probity of this decision. Lizzie's attorney, Andrew Jennings, asked that the judge recuse himself since he had already heard the inquest testimony and therefore was prejudiced. Judge Blaisdel declined to disqualify himself, causing himself to be blasted from the pulpit and pilloried in the press (Sullivan, 49).

Now begins the period of Lizzie Borden's greatest popularity. During the inquest, the preliminary hearing, the grand jury hearing and the trial for murder, Lizzie became the favorite of several ministries, a cause celebre of the burgeoning women's movement and the darling of a variety of big city newsrooms up and down the eastern seaboard. News reporters from all over Massachusetts, as well as Boston, New York and Baltimore, converged on Fall River hoping to get a scoop. Usually, all they got was the tableau of Lizzie supported by her two faithful clergymen, Reverend Jubb and Reverend Buck. These men of the cloth led the parade of supporters including members of the Women's Christian Temperance Movement Suffragettes and the Women's Auxiliary of the YMCA (Pearson, 232-233).

Unfortunately, the lull of information during the week between the murders and the inquest became so maddening to the men of the fourth estate that desperate, unsubstantiated rumors made their way into headlines. The Trickey affair is a case in point. Edwin D. McHenry was a private detective who sold to a trusting young reporter named Trickey the big scoop: the names of the witnesses to be called in the grand jury hearing, along with the revelation that Lizzie Borden was--pregnant! According to one witness, Andrew Borden had been heard shouting, "I will know the name of the man who got you in trouble (Lincoln, 222)!" The *Boston Globe,* upon McHenry's urging, published the news without checking the facts. In 24 hours they were printing retractions. The names on the list that McHenry gave Trickey were fraudulent, and by implication the news of Lizzie's nascent motherhood was, too. Trickey ran across the Canadian border to escape prosecution and was promptly run over by a train. The *Boston Globe* apologized profusely to Miss Borden in print and remained a friend to her throughout her legal proceedings (Sullivan, 18 - 191). On the other hand, the *Fall River Daily Globe,* seeing itself as the defender of the people, blasted the Bordens as elitist oppressors of the poor (Reach, 60). From the publicity engendered by these two views, the Borden case gained great notoriety in the U.S. and abroad from the inquest, six days after the murders, to the trial 10 months later.

On November 7, 1892, the grand jury was assembled to determine if sufficient evidence had been gathered to warrant a trial by jury. The hearing lasted until November 21, when the grand jury reconvened to hear the testimony of Miss Alice Russell, Lizzie's friend and confidante on the night before the murders. Upon this new testimony, three indictments were returned against Lizzie Borden: one charged her with the murder of Andrew Borden, the second charged her with the murder of Abby Borden and the third charged her with the murder of both (Sullivan, 55).

What was the additional testimony that Lizzie's friend Alice Russell offered? It was the news of a burned dress. One of the great mysteries of the Borden case is how Lizzie committed the crimes (if, indeed, she did) without spilling blood upon herself and her clothes. From the time Lizzie first called Bridget downstairs and sent her for a doctor to the time the police arrived, Lizzie was clean and tidy. Furthermore, no blood-stained dress of Lizzie's was ever found. However, on December 1, Alice Russell testified that three days after the murders she was fixing breakfast at the Bordens' for Lizzie and Emma, and when she went into the kitchen she saw Lizzie at the stove with the remains of a dress in her hand. Emma Borden, who was at the kitchen sink, turned to Lizzie and asked what she was going to do. Lizzie answered, "I'm going to burn this old thing up. It is covered with paint." Alice Russell told her, "I'm afraid, Lizzie, that the worst thing you could have done was to burn that dress. I have been asked about your dresses." To this, Lizzie exclaimed, "Oh, what made you let me do it (Sullivan, 100-101)?"

Miss Russell's last-minute revelation was only a foretaste of what was to come the following June. The murder trial itself was filled with humor, histrionics and surprising upsets. Of the three presiding justices, Mason, Blodgett and Dewey, Albert Mason was chief justice. Justice Justin Dewey proved the most notorious with his infamously loaded summation to the jury. The attorneys for the defense were the best money could buy: Andrew J. Jennings of local prominence in Fall River, Melvin O. Adams of Boston and the Honorable George D. Robinson, governor emeritus of Massachusetts (1884-1887). While Lizzie Borden enjoyed the services of three distinguished attorneys, the Commonwealth of Massachusetts was ably represented with two distinguished prosecuting attorneys: Hosea M. Knowlton and William H. Moody. Knowlton himself was a reluctant litigator, almost apologetic in the prosecution of the state's case against Lizzie. On the other hand, Moody was a dynamic young lawyer who would rise in time to the Supreme Court of the United States. Moody provided the pyrotechnics in the opening statement so forcefully that the defendant fainted. After holding up the dress offered as evidence, Moody tossed it on the table with a flourish, knocking over an open handbag from which two skulls fell out. According to Joseph Howard of the *Boston Globe:*

> *The sight of those skulls was pregnant with meaning and Mr.*
> *Moody's description of their gashed and hacked mutilations must*
> *have intensified the vividness of the scene to the inner conscious-*
> *ness of the prisoner who then without sigh, or gasp, or convulsive*
> *movement, dropped her head and slid upon her official companion,*
> *her face blue red with congestive symptoms, an inert, consciousless*
> *mass of inanimate flesh (Sullivan, 76).*

These skulls mysteriously vanished shortly after the trial, never to be seen again. Recently, forensic scientist James E. Starrs claimed to have discovered the whereabouts of the skulls. Using radar, he has located what appears to be the missing skulls "about three feet above the rest of the remains of the Bordens," in Fall River's Oak Grove Cemetery (Stuart, A-8). Whoever stole the skulls remains a mystery.

With the skulls holding everyone's attention, the Prosecution in its opening statement promised the jury that it would show that the accused had a predisposition to commit murder, the exclusive opportunity to commit the murders and the consciousness of guilt afterwards in the lies she told. The first witnesses for the Prosecution were minor ones: an engineer and photographer who testified as to the layout of the house and photographs of the murder victims. Then Uncle John Morse took the stand. Uncle John was not much help to either the Prosecution or the Defense. He was too vague on detail, not even knowing Lizzie's correct age. Morse did cause the courtroom to break out in laughter when the Defense asked him if it had been a good breakfast served to him on that hot August morning. "Plenty of it!" he affirmed (Radin, 113). However, he caused a shudder through the courtroom with his description of Abby Borden's corpse: "I went up far enough so I could look under the bed where I slept the night before, and I saw Mrs. Borden lying there with blood on her face (Radin, 112)."

Following Uncle John Morse were witnesses establishing the time period when Andrew Borden was in town on business. Shortsleeves and Mather testified to his odd behavior in picking up the broken lock. Once these preliminaries were out of the way, key witnesses began to give conflicting testimonies on key evidence concerning the two-piece dress, the hatchet and the heat in the barn.

Bridget Sullivan, Lizzie's maid whom she called "Maggie," was called several times to the witness stand where she gave often confusing and conflicting testimony. At one point, she completely denied testimony she had given in the inquest about the family's eating habits (Radin, 120). Also, she hedged many of her statements to avoid saying anything definite. According to Sullivan, "Bridget then said that she never did say that Lizzie was crying at any time. Notwithstanding a plain inference by Robinson, the cross-examiner, that she had made the statement at the inquest, Bridget insisted that she had not (92)." Many years later in Butte, Montana, Bridget supposedly made a deathbed confession to Minnie Green, her old friend from Ireland. Bridget told her friend that she had received money from Lizzie in exchange for her help at the trial. According to Lincoln:

> *She had always liked Lizzie; she told Minnie she had always felt herself on the girl's side in the dimly understood troubles in that house. So she helped her out in the trial. And still she had not said one single word that was not true, not a word. Lizzie was thankful to her, and Lizzie's lawyer made her promise to stay in Ireland and never come back (313).*

Considering her circumlocutions on the witness stand, one only wonders what Bridget withheld. Testifying that "she never did say that Lizzie was crying" is not the same as saying Lizzie cried, just as "not saying one single word was not true" is not the same as telling the truth.

There is no better example of Bridget's blarney than her testimony concerning the dress that Lizzie wore the day of the murders. Not only could none of the principals agree upon the dress, even Borden experts cannot agree upon the testimony given. Pearson writes, "All of these witnesses were questioned about the dress which Miss Borden was wearing when they first saw her after the murders. Dr. Bowen's testimony was confused. Mrs. Churchill described it as 'a light blue and white ground work, with a dark navy blue diamond on it (Pearson, 248)." Officer Mullaly testified, "I thought she had on a light blue. I thought there was a small figure on the dress, a little spot, like (Sullivan, 113)." These two witnesses described, in essence, the dress Alice Russell saw Lizzie burn. On the other hand, the doctor's wife, Phoebe Bowen, identified the dark blue dress Lizzie had given to the police as the one worn the morning of the murders (Radin, 168). Bridget's own answer to the question differs depending on which expert is read. According to Lincoln, Bridget hedged, "It wasn't a calico that the girl was in the habit of wearing mornings (236)." Edward Radin records Bridget's response to be, "No, sir, I couldn't tell what dress the girl had on (117)." But Robert Sullivan reports Bridget saying, "Lizzie was wearing at that time a blue dress with a sprig in it. It was light blue. The sprig was darker blue than the dress (85)." By all accounts the dress Sullivan has Bridget describing was the Bedford cord Alice Russell watched Lizzie burn. Yet, incredibly, this evidence was completely ignored by the Prosecution, the judges, later experts and even Robert Sullivan, who records it without comment.

The confusion over the dress is no doubt understandable, considering the witnesses were asked to recall a detail from 10 months earlier. Another reason might be that *both* dresses were worn. Lincoln suggests that, "A woman with a terrible reason to hide the blue 'wrapper' might have been driven by desperation to put on a winter party dress in which to go out that hot day and establish her alibi simply because it also was two-piece (93-94)." Lizzie-- dressing partly in cheap, light blue cotton and partly in dark, expensive silk-- had baffled them all, including Bridget.

If Bridget allowed herself to be misled, she was not the only one. Dr. Bowen was another sympathetic bystander, very much involved in impeding the investigation, especially by manning the door to Lizzie's bedroom when the police wished to search the premises. At the trial, Deputy Marshall John Fleet testified:

> *'I went to Lizzie's door, rapped on the door; Dr. Bowen came to it,
> holding the door, opening the door, I should say about six inches,
> and asked what was wanted. I told him we had come there as po-
> lice officers to search this room and search the building. He then
> turned around to Miss Borden and told me to wait a moment. He
> then opened the door again and said that Lizzie wanted to know if
> it was absolutely necessary for us to search that room. I told him,
> murders having been committed, it was our duty so to do, and we
> wanted to get in there. He closed the door again and said some-
> thing to Miss Borden, and finally opened the door and admitted
> us (Sullivan, 106).'*

John Fleet's testimony creates a striking picture. The doctor, cracking the door
open only wide enough to stick out his nose, was obviously attempting to
keep the police from looking inside. Was Lizzie changing clothes during the
three times the doctor delayed the police from entering? What were they hid-
ing that they did not want the police to see? Such stalling would seem comical
if Dr. Bowen had not been later caught downstairs destroying evidence.

One of the most baffling pieces of missing evidence is the mysterious note
Abby supposedly received from a sick friend. That was what Lizzie told Bridget, her father and Mrs. Adelaide Churchill; however, no note was ever found.
Even after the Borden sisters posted a $5,000 reward for information about the
note, no one came forward to help or collect the money. Neither the messen-
ger nor the invalid letter writer were heard from again. The most obvious ex-
planation for the disappearing note is that no note was sent; it was just a
pretext of Lizzie's to keep others from discovering Abby Borden's body too
soon. However,one police officer saw Dr. Bowen burn a rolled-up piece of
paper. According to Captain Harrington:

> *'Then I went to the kitchen, and while I was in the kitchen,
> just as I went to pass by Dr. Bowen, between him and the
> stove, I saw some scraps of note paper in his hand. I asked
> him what they were and he said, 'Oh, I guess it is nothing.' I
> saw the word 'Emma' in the left-hand corner. I asked Dr.
> Bowen what about the paper, what it contained, and he said,
> 'I think it is nothing. It is something, I think, about my*

> *daughter going through somewhere.' Then he turned slightly to his
> left, took the lid from the stove, and threw the paper in--or the
> pieces in. I looked in the fire, and I saw that there had been paper
> burned there before. It was rolled up and still held a cylindrical
> form. The roll of paper was about twelve inches long, I should say,
> and not over two inches wide* (Sullivan, 111-112).'

What Harrington saw might well have been a strip of scrap paper on which
the missing note from the mysterious friend was written. Why Dr. Bowen
would wish to destroy it is another mystery. Victoria Lincoln believes Bowen
found the incriminating papers the Prosecution hoped to find locked in
old Andrew's safe (126-127). Many Borden scholars believe that what
Bowen burned, wrapped in paper, was in fact none other than the handle to the infamous hatchet that sent both Andrew and Abby Borden to
their deaths (Radin, 138).

The strange-looking object that the Prosecution presented as the murder
weapon was a handleless hatchet found the day of the murders in the
Borden basement, the head smeared with ash. According to Officer
Michael Mullaly:

> *'I went with Bridget down to the cellar, looking for the hatchets and
> axes. Bridget led the way. Went to the cellar and she took from a
> box two hatchets. I saw the hatchet which Mr. Fleet took-- or the
> part of the hatchet;* [the witness is shown the hatchet] *it looked
> very much like it, only the break was cleaner. It looked at the time
> as though it was just broken; it looked like a fresh break. It was cov-
> ered with dust and ashes or something like that. The handle was
> broken fresh. Both sides of it were covered with ashes, both sides of
> the blade, that is* (Sullivan, 113-114).'

This hatchet blade was later inspected by Suffolk County Medical Examiner
Dr. Frank Draper, Professor of Medical Jurisprudence at Harvard Medical
School. He testified, "It is both the length of the hatchet and the thinness of the
edge of the blade at certain places in this individual handleless hatchet that led
me to the opinion that this handleless hatchet could inflict these wounds
which I have observed (Sullivan, 132)." Dr. Draper testified only normal
strength was needed to inflict the violent blows to the head both Bordens suffered. He said, "The inflicting of these blows was within the physical capabil-
ity of an average woman of average strength (Sullivan, 132)."

So far, so good. The Prosecution had done much to establish the handle-less hatchet as the murder weapon and indicated that it could be wielded by a woman like Lizzie to do the damage that was done. That it was han-dleless and smeared with ashes also seemed incriminating, as if someone had attempted to disguise it. All was going well until Officer Mullaly resumed his testimony. Under Defense Attorney Robinson's cross examina-tion, Mullaly mentioned that there was another piece in the box along with the hatchet.

"Was it the handle to a hatchet?" the defense attorney asked. Mullaly replied, "It was what I call a hatchet handle. It was somewhat shorter than the handles of the other hatchets." At this point Robinson asked District Attorney Knowl-ton, "The Government does not know where it is?" Shamefaced, Knowlton answered, "I do not know where it is. This is the first time I ever heard of it." Robinson, turning back to his witness, asked Mullaly, "Did you ever tell any-one of this before?" The inexplicable reply was, "No, sir, I never did (Sullivan, 114-115)."

The Prosecution called the capable Deputy Marshall Fleet back to the stand to testify that he had never seen the broken handle in the box with the hatchet blade or anywhere else. Nevertheless, the damage had already been done. Doubt was sown into the minds of the 12 jurors whether the handleless hatchet was indeed the murder weapon or just a broken tool left discarded in the basement.

With disagreement over the dress and confusion over the hatchet, the Prose-cution was left with Lizzie's alibi of being in the barn when her father's mur-der took place. On the face of it, the alibi was so preposterous that it seemed almost a confession of guilt. What an amazing coincidence that a daughter who had not fished in years would choose to go to the barn to hunt for sinkers and subsequently stay to eat pears in the hayloft during a heat wave for the exact 20 minutes in which her father was being bludgeoned to death! Further-more, the police, who had been less than thorough in checking the house, were very efficient in searching the barn. Once more, the competent Deputy Marshall Fleet took the stand. He testified to having gone to the barn and find-ing it hot as well as undisturbed. It seemed unlikely that anyone had been eat-ing in the loft and even unlikelier that anyone would want to. According to Sullivan, "Fleet's testimony of the extreme heat in the barn loft was significant as bearing upon the falsity of Lizzie's story of having remained there for about half an hour on the day of the murders (109)."

> *'It was very dusty there, very uninviting; the floor, bench, and hay and old fashioned fireplace which stood in the west-end corner and some windows were covered with dust. The windows were all closed and were covered with cobwebs. It was very disagreeable breathing there because of the dust. It was suffocating hot (Sullivan, 112).'*

Perhaps the most damning testimony of all was from Inspector William H. Medley, who actually went up into the loft and found only his own footsteps in the dust. He said:

> *'I stooped down low to see if I could discern any marks on the floor of the barn having been made there I didn't see any, and I reached out my hand to see if I could make an impression on the floor of the barn, and I did by putting my hand down so fashion, and found that I made an impression (Sullivan, 119-120).'*

Once the Prosecution finished, there seemed little doubt that Lizzie Borden had not been in the hayloft; the hayloft was found to be too hot and too undisturbed for her alibi to be believed. The inference must be drawn that she lied about being in the barn to hide her real whereabouts that morning. However, the Defense introduced three witnesses of their own whose testimony undermined even that of the Fall River Police.

An ice cream vendor named Hyman Lubinsky took the stand. He was an immigrant who spoke English with a thick accent and could barely follow the questions put to him. Nevertheless, he was able to say confidently that he was driving his wagon down Second Street "a few minutes after eleven" and saw "a lady come out the way from the barn right to the stairs at the back of the house. She wore a dark dress, had nothing on her head, and she was walking slowly. I have seen the servant girl there before, and this woman was not the servant (Sullivan, 150)." So Lizzie had indeed gone to the barn, according to Lubinsky, and she was wearing a dark blue dress, not the light blue Bedford cord Alice Russell saw her burn. This testimony was damaging to the Prosecution's case, and District Attorney Knowlton was not at all cordial in cross-examining the simple tradesman. Several times Lubinsky had to protest, "You ask me too fast!" Julian Ralph of the *New York Sun* wrote, "Never did a lawyer try harder to confuse a witness than did Mr. Knowlton on this occasion (Radin, 154)." With a tone described as "nervous and querulous," Knowlton seemed almost censorious that Lubinsky should see anything at all. "What has a person got eyes for, but to look with?" Lubinsky told him (Pearson, 254). Although Knowlton failed to shake the testimony of the ice cream vendor, the Prosecution fared better with Charles E. Gardner, who had fed Lubinsky's horses and followed him 15 minutes later down Second Street. This would put the time that Gardner passed the Borden house at 11:30, yet Gardner testified that he saw no activity there. Knowlton pointed out to the jury that if, in fact, Gardner's reckoning of the time were correct, he would have seen a lot of activity going on there (Sullivan, 150).

This line of questioning seemed to be effective in destroying both witnesses' sense of time, and perhaps would have dispelled any doubts as to the absurdity of the barn alibi, if it were not for "Me and Brownie." Everett Brown and Thomas Barlow were two young truants from school who stumbled upon the murder scene and were consequently given their day in court. They were known in the newspapers as "Me and Brownie," since that was the way Barlow referred to himself and his friend. Barlow lived three blocks away from the Bordens, on Third Street. He and his chum were "fooling along" or pushing each other off the sidewalk until they happened upon the scene of the crime. On a dare, they sneaked back to the barn and went up to the loft where they stayed five minutes. Barlow swore under oath, "Me and Brownie went in the side gate, went to the barn and up to the hayloft. It was cooler in the barn than outside (Sullivan, 151)." Once down from the loft, they were spotted by the authorities and escorted from the premises. District Attorney Knowlton was not pleased. "The barn loft was a nice, comfortable, cool place?" he challenged in cross examination. The prompt answer came, "Yes, sir" (Pearson, 255), and the third leg of Knowlton's prosecution was pulled out from under him.

Though a burr in the prosecuting attorney's side, Me and Brownie were quite the darlings of the press. Even Edmund Pearson, writing in 1924, felt inspired by the boys to pen this rhapsodic apostrophe:

> *Ah, 'Me and Brownie,' the rest of the folk who were in the New Bedford Court House that day are either dead, or they are old, old people. But you are not too old to recall with delight the day you had a trip over from Fall River, and a free ride on the train, chummed with the police, and for awhile stood with the fierce light of fame beating upon you, the reporters taking down your words, to be printed that*

evening in the papers. What mattered to you if Truth blushed and turned aside while you spoke (Pearson, 255)?

In defense of Brown and Barlow, who insisted the hayloft was cool when Lizzie admitted it was hot, Lizzie also testified she opened the hayloft window. If the boys had come after the investigators, a breeze might have cooled the loft, making the barn seem relatively inviting. Whether Me and Brownie lied or not, their testimony, coupled with Lubinsky, discredited the Prosecution. The boys made Lizzie's alibi plausible, and the ice cream vendor corroborated it and identified her in the dark dress.

His circumstantial evidence badly shaken, Prosecutor Knowlton in his closing argument had to rely upon the impossibility of another outside attacker:

> '*He came into the house where there was no chance to get in, he hid in closets where no blood was found, he went from room to room where no traces of blood were found in passageways or stairs, he came out when there was no opportunity to come out without being seen by all the world, that unknown assassin who knew all the ins and outs of the family, who knew Bridget Sullivan was going upstairs to sleep when she didn't know it herself, who knew when Lizzie was going to the barn when she didn't know it herself, who knew that Mrs. Borden would be up there dusting the guest room when no person could have foreseen it, who knew that he could get through and escape the eye of Lizzie and would find that screen door open at the exact time when it was possible to run in; that unknown assassin never would have carried the weapon away, never would have carried the blood weapon with him into the streets. It would have been left beside his victims. The fact that no hatchet was found there is itself evidence. Would the unknown assassin have written the note? To have his victim leave the house? That note was never sent. The note was never written* (Sullivan, 171)!'

Inspector Medley

While the Prosecution relied upon common sense and reason, the Defense appealed to the sentiment and common decency of the jurors. Sullivan writes:

> *Robinson, after reminding the jury that 'The eyes that can not*
> *weep are the saddest eyes of all,' and that Andrew Borden had gone*
> *to his grave wearing on his hand the symbol of 'the pledge of faith*
> *and love, the ring which belonged to his little girl* [Lizzie],' *he*
> *pointed to the defendant, then shouted, 'To find her guilty, you*
> *must believe her to be a fiend! Does she look it* (Sullivan, 168)?'

The Defense rested. Luckily for Lizzie, her attorney, George D. Robinson, had once been governor and brought enormous prestige to her cause. It also helped that the judge, Justice Justin Dewey, was appointed to the Superior Court when Robinson was governor. There has been much speculation on the propriety of the judge hearing the case. After the trial, Judge Charles G. Davis wrote that "Judge Dewey's charge was a better and more effective argument upon the facts in favor of Lizzie Borden than that delivered by Lizzie's own counsel (Sullivan, 172)." In Justice Dewey's charge to the jury, he praised Lizzie's character as "one of positive, of active benevolence in religious and charitable work." He cautioned the jury not to heed hearsay rumors of Lizzie speaking ill of Abby, "remembering it is the language of a young woman and not of a philosopher." And he advised that "the evidence, consisting as it does in the mere repetition of oral statements, is subject to much imperfection and mistake (Sullivan, 173-174)"

As for Lizzie, throughout the long, hot trial she remained silent, unwilling to testify for--or possibly against--herself. Finally, at the trial's end, Lizzie was asked if she had anything to say in her own behalf. With a cold, hard stare at the jury she announced, "I am innocent. I leave it to my counsel to speak for me (Sullivan, 171)."

That was that! Lizzie was acquitted on the first ballot. The jury needed only an hour and a half to find her not guilty before adjourning to a local saloon for beers (Lincoln, 229). Lizzie promptly held a reception for her gentlemen friends of the press (299), and the police announced they were suspending the investigation of the deaths (Sullivan, 205). That year Edwin Porter published *The Fall River Tragedy*. All copies were bought and suppressed by Lizzie Borden (Lincoln, 304). It did not take long for the world to wonder: if Lizzie did not do it, who did? To this day, Lizzie remains the most likely suspect, yet the blatant brutality of the crimes argues against her guilt. As Lincoln says:

> *It was so forthright, so downright masculine, that a carefully se-*
> *lected jury of nice old men could barely give serious thought to*
> *the possibility that a well-brought-up young lady could have*
> *been the murderer--though they would have thought hard about*
> *that acceptable, womanly prussic acid* (Lincoln, 45).

Or, to put it another way:

> *There's no evidence of guilt, Lizzie Borden*
> *That should make your spirit wilt, Lizzie Borden;*
> *Many do not think that you*
> *Chopped your father's head in two,*
> *It's so hard a thing to do, Lizzie Borden.*
> -- A.L. Bixby

■   ■   ■

The Borden Jury

Chapter 11

THE KEY

Although judged not guilty in a court of law, Lizzie Borden was judged not innocent by the public and served out a life sentence as a social pariah in Fall River. Since her time, scholars have studied and researched and learned many of the details of the Borden case, yet two of the three most important facts are self-evident, while the elusive third remains a mystery. All know when the murders took place; most agree how they took place. No one, however, knows why. A new will in Abby Borden's favor might explain the violent deaths, yet no will was found. Likewise, there was no thwarted love interest to make the crime one of passion, as the Trickey news report indicated and as Agnes DeMille's ballet, "Fall River Legend," suggests. Perhaps the heat of that long hot spell provides the impetus for violence--but surely not for the motivation of violence. Why stop with two deaths before killing the maid as well?

The key to Lizzie Borden's motivation can be found in the very details she told to friends and authorities at the time of the murders, and in her testimony at the inquest. If Lizzie were indeed the murderess, then her alibi was a tissue of lies in which the selection of details reveals much about her subconscious mind. Victoria Lincoln earlier commented on Lizzie's mind as "so unimaginative and so wholly out of touch with reality (Lincoln, 172)." Lincoln refers to Lizzie's lying to the authorities as, "this tic, combined with her compulsion to mention and explain away incriminating details (172)." Lincoln explains, "While Lizzie could not invent details, little touches to give a story life and credibility, she was overmastered by actual details, unnoticeable details which she is driven to mention and explain away (171)."

An examination of the key details in Lizzie's version of what happened unlocks the compulsions and delusions that led to the murders. These key details fall into three general groups. The poison, the break-ins and the note indicated Lizzie's coded messages for help. The vermin, the burglars and the pears in the barn reveal her subconscious fears and frustrations. The locks, the handleless hatchet and the two-piece dress are left as elements in an allegorical psychodrama. The drama was played out not only by Lizzie's compulsions, but by the compulsions of Andrew and Abby Borden. They, too, participated in the symbolic action of Lizzie's purification ceremony, and there is a bloody poetry and mad poetic justice at the bottom of these crude, senseless crimes that have made the Fall River murders legendary.

Consider the coincidence of Abby and Lizzie both telling neighbors that they were being poisoned on the day before the murders. Also, consider the coincidence of Abby going to Dr. Bowen on the pretext of receiving a note from an anonymous friend warning her of being poisoned. Then the next day she is gone, supposedly upon the pretext of receiving a note from an unknown friend who was sick. The sick friend was none other than Lizzie herself. Lizzie told Alice Russell the night before the murders, "I am afraid somebody will do something (Sullivan, 99)." Lizzie was afraid because there *was* a note; it was the note Abby invented to confide her fears in Dr. Bowen across the street. Neither Lizzie nor Andrew wanted Abby to leave the house. Andrew was heard shouting when she left that no money of his would pay for her doctor's visit, even though both had been very ill. Lizzie, too, did not want Abby to leave spreading tales, so she silenced her the very next day--but not with poison. Lizzie always maintained that she did not try to buy poison from the druggist. Poison was not Lizzie's way. Besides, the poisoning had already begun, and Lizzie feared it as much as Abby. The poison she feared was not prussic acid, but something darker--so dark that it could only be described as poison.

Poison complexes are not uncommon. Noted psychologist R. Emil Gutheil identifies a poison complex as a "group of ideas in which concern about being poisoned or poisoning others is expressed (636)." Gutheil explains that the "poison delusion corresponds to the idea that sexual preoccupation with the person is poisoning his mind (460)." Often in this delusion the patient equates poisoning with fertilization. Therefore, fear of pregnancy, not poison, is paramount (Gutheil, 154). However, neither Abby nor Lizzie should have had any fear of becoming pregnant.

Nevertheless, Freud points out that the subconscious mind reveals itself through symbols and warns not to confuse dream symbols with dream content. Just as Lizzie revealed her subconscious fears by saying she was being poisoned, so Lizzie reveals the nature of these fears in her references to vermin at the inquest.

At the inquest, Druggist Eli Bence testified that Lizzie wanted the poison to kill moths infesting her sealskin cape. Compare this detail with Lizzie's answer when quizzed about a spot of blood on her petticoat: "I have fleas." Some read in her answer a Victorian delicacy to speak euphemistically about her menstrual period (Lincoln, 214). However, Lizzie was normally too blunt for euphemism. Having fleas seems no more delicate than having her menstrual period. Also, Lizzie seems too competent to attempt purchasing poison that could not be sold without a doctor's prescription. She claimed in her inquest testimony that, "I did not go to Smith's drug store to buy prussic acid (Sullivan, 216)." Just as her asking for prussic acid was a coded message for help, her references to vermin are a message from her subconscious mind. Flea bites in dreams symbolize pangs of conscience, Gutheil explains. "Insects may be also interpreted as obsessive thoughts. In the conscience, reactions to such thoughts are directed against the patient's own ego, as are the bites of animals directed against his body. Bugs, also [are] those cases where the dreamer is persistently fighting against them and they keep on oppressing him (171)." Lizzie's fear of poison and vermin indicate revulsion against obsessive thoughts--perhaps of an erotic nature.

Further circumstantial evidence of Lizzie's repressed sexuality can be seen in her alibi of eating pears in the sweltering barn. Dr. Gutheil identifies the barn as a symbol of the female sexual organs (150), while a pear is symbolic of the phallus (138). According to Freud, a fish is also a phallic symbol (373). Therefore, the alibi of eating pears in the stifling hot hayloft after going to the barn for fishing gear suggests a series of erotic thoughts repressed in the unconscious through dream symbolism. Remember, in Lizzie's own testimony she stated, "I have told you everything that took place up in the barn. It was the hottest place in the premises. I went to the barn because the irons were not hot enough and the fire had gone out (Sullivan, 217)." Here is a striking picture of a spinster during a hot spell, driven not so much by the heat, but by the lack of heat, to while away her time in a fancy silk dress, eating pears in the hayloft of an empty barn.

If, indeed, Lizzie Borden repressed these sexual thoughts out of fear, the inevitable question is, Why? The answer to her repressed sexual fear can be found in her expressed fear of the dark stranger. According to Officer Mullaly's testimony at the trial, Lizzie told him, "she saw a man around there sometimes before with dark clothes on (Sullivan, 114)." Lizzie herself said at the inquest, "One night as I was coming home not long ago I saw the shadow of a man on the house at the east end. I saw somebody run around the house last winter (217)." Compare these statements with the fear Lizzie expressed to Alice Russell the night before the killings: "I feel as if I wanted to sleep with my eyes half open--with one eye half open all the time--for fear they will burn the house down over us (99)." The fear of dark strangers breaking into houses at night while the occupants are asleep is a common one. According to Freud, "Robbers, burglars, and ghosts, of which we are afraid before going to bed, originate in one and the same childish reminiscence. They are nightly visitors who have waked the child, the robbers were always the father (Freud, 397)." As for the father, Alice Russell claimed that Lizzie was afraid "Somebody will do something because he is so discourteous (99)." Andrew Borden was described in many ways: cheap, stingy, hard. But discourteous? In all the anecdotes told of the man, none illustrate a want of courtesy. What was his discourtesy? And whom had he offended?

Here we should consider the father's role in the psychodrama of his own murder. Andrew Borden was more than a passive victim in his own death; he was an active--even willing--participant. To understand that, we must consider the escalating family feud that had started a year earlier--not between Abby and Lizzie as has been supposed, but between Lizzie and Andrew.

According to Bridget Sullivan's testimony, the Bordens' home had been burglarized 12 months before the murders, shortly after Lizzie's return from her continental tour when she moved into Emma's room. The feud began in earnest when someone rifled through Abby's things. Abby's things were a paltry lot: some cheap jewelry, petty cash and a book of streetcar tickets were taken (Sullivan, 92). Andrew Borden reported the matter to the police, although such a burglary seemed impossible, occurring as it did in the daytime while the house was locked from the inside and occupied by Emma, Lizzie and Bridget (according to Alice Russell's trial testimony).

Supposedly, Lizzie took a suspiciously enthusiastic interest in the police investigation. Victoria Lincoln writes, "Miss Lizzie Borden was over-excited. She talked incessantly, taking the police to the cellar to show them how she had found the door unbolted and a large nail stuck in the keyhole, which they put down in their records as 'an eight or ten penny nail (Lincoln, 51).'" Lizzie's odd behavior, as well as the bizarre evidence she discovered, "convinced the police and Andrew Borden that Lizzie herself might have planned and set the robbery scene (Sullivan, 92)." The investigation was dropped at Andrew's request, but thereafter he made a habit of locking his wife's and his bedroom door and placing the key prominently on the mantelpiece--the same mantel where he placed the disused lock he had picked up the day he died.

Several commentators have remarked on this practice as an exercise in amateur psychology (see Lincoln and Sullivan). If this be the case, what would be the symbolic message of the locked door and the accessible key? In The Interpretation of Dreams, Sigmund Freud states explicitly that "a room in a dream generally represents a woman," adding that "the question as to whether the room is 'open' or 'locked' will be readily understood," so that "there is no need to be explicit as to the sort of key that will unlock the room (371-372)." However, elsewhere in this landmark text of psychology, Freud is explicit when he states that "penetration into narrow spaces and the opening of locked doors are among the commonest of sexual symbols (392)."

Whether or not Andrew Borden intended to send a message with such a sexual subtext is debatable, but Lizzie's ten-penny nail stuck in the basement lock seems eerily symbolic of sexual violation. The "robbery" and her "discovery" of this peculiar clue could well have comprised a signal of some fear too deep to verbalize that could only be acted out subconsciously. The acting out of the subconscious becomes a psychodrama with father and daughter playing opposite each other.

Both parties now joined, the family feud escalates. Twice, the barn is broken into at night--once in the fall and again in the spring, according to Bridget Sullivan's testimony (Sullivan, 92). The break-ins were mostly a nuisance; nothing of value was taken. Indeed, nothing of value was kept in the barn except for Lizzie's pigeons. Then in March, Andrew retaliated and decapitated the birds with a hatchet (Lincoln, 56). At the inquest, Lizzie recalled asking at the time, "Why are their

Lizzie Borden as a Child

heads off (194)?" This happened only one season away from the brutal murders of Abby and Andrew Borden in which they were struck down 19 and 11 times, respectively, with a hatched aimed only at their heads--while daughter Lizzie was supposedly out in the violated barn where her pet pigeons had died. The missing heads of the pigeons and the bludgeoned heads of the parents were all struck by a hatchet, no doubt the same hatchet that later itself was decapitated, leaving only the head of the blade smeared with ashes. Freud states, "It is quite unmistakable that all weapons and tools are used as symbols for the male organ (373)." On the subconscious level, therefore, the decapitated hatchet might well be symbolic fulfillment for a castration wish.

Again, the careful reader must ask, Why? There can be no actual evidence of subconscious activity, only circumstantial evidence. For it is by the dream symbols that the dream content is interpreted. With this in mind, Lizzie's unaccountable laugh on the stairs might be explained. As mentioned earlier, one of the more bizarre aspects of the case was Lizzie's sudden laugh when her father was at the door. Some interpret it as her grisly delight at the victim's arrival. Others see it merely as a response to the maid's mild oath, "Pshaw," when she was unable to open the door. However, considering the enormous psychological role that locks played in that most dysfunctional of all dysfunctional families, perhaps Lizzie laughed at the irony of her father being locked out.

One must consider how thoroughly locked up the Bordens were in their own home. The front door with which Bridget was having trouble as Mr. Borden arrived had three separate locks that had to be released before it would open (Sullivan, 84). Likewise, when Deputy Marshal Fleet began his preliminary investigation minutes after the second murder, he discovered the Bordens' bedroom locked (105). Furthermore, there were two newspaper reporters from the *Fall River Globe* and *Fall River News* who were also poking about the home and found the cellar door locked as well (Sullivan, 102). Only the screen door, which was usually locked, remained open during the time of the murders. Significantly, Lizzie first told Miss Russell that she went to the barn to get a piece of tin or iron to fix her screen, although later investigation found no screen "loose or in other than perfect shape (Lincoln, 109)." Concerning a patient's dream about breaking through a locked door, Dr. Gutheil sees "this dream 'materially' as concern about the possible consequences of a sexual act (60)." Again, the subconscious symbolism suggests a sexual act but does not indicate with whom. There was one more locked door recorded in Deputy Marshal Fleet's report, which may shed light upon this pervasive dream. Fleet reports:

> 'We searched her [Lizzie's] room and as we came to the head of her bed I found a door there and went to open it. She said that door was locked and bolted from the other side and we could not go through there, and I found that it was locked on her side. The door was hooked with a common hook and staple (Sullivan, 106).'

This door, which Lizzie declared was locked and bolted, is noteworthy in that it was only hooked by a latch, unlike the other doors through the house, which contained spring locks. Victoria Lincoln's description of Lizzie's room indicates with which room that door communicated. She writes that the room was "sunny, with two windows to the south; but five doors and two windows in a modest-sized room leave little wall space. A heavy secretary-desk with a bookcase top stood against the locked door to the guest room, and the washstand stood cater cornered with a portiere hung before it (50)." Of the five doors, three could be opened (to the hallway, to the closet and to Emma's room). Only two were "locked": the door to the guest room, which was hidden by the large secretary, and the door to old Andrew's room, which was latched with a hook in a staple. If the story of Lizzie killing Abby's cat is true, perhaps she killed it not out of spite, but out of fear that the cat might sometime unhook that door. The room had been Emma's, but Emma was only too willing to give it to Lizzie and take instead the smaller room that could only be reached through Lizzie's. The sisters switched rooms shortly before the strange series of break-ins that concluded with the murders of Andrew and Abby Borden.

Lizzie Borden has been described as "a New England spinster, prim, virginal, ingrown, affluent, who one day suddenly runs berserk, commits two unspeakable crimes, and against all the laws of probability, gets away with them, then reverts to her former state and lives out the remainder of her long life in Spartan silence (Reach, 64)." If this is true, perhaps the greatest mystery is that so many people close to her, who must have known, would keep silence and tacitly become accomplices. Why did not Emma, or Bridget or Dr. Bowen speak out? What circumstances could possibly mitigate such a crime in favor of the perpetrator? Perhaps those close to Lizzie were able to understand and sympathize with her violence--as they were able to condone her compulsive stealing. In 1897, Lizzie was accused of shoplifting. In Providence, Rhode Island, Tilden and Thurber, Jewelers, swore out a warrant for Lizzie's arrest for shoplifting two small porcelain figurines called *Love's Dream* and *Love's Awakening* (Lincoln, 305). The petty thefts from Mrs. Borden's room, the break-ins at the barn, now shoplifting--all show a pattern of compulsive stealing, or kleptomania. Often, the act of theft in cases of kleptomania substitutes for a forbidden sexual act--often incest (Gutheil, 467).

Furthermore, Dr. Gutheil comments, "It is not sufficiently known that behind kleptomania often a much more serious impulse may be hidden than that of sexual aggression: the impulse of murder (469)." The titles of the figurines symbolize the beginning and the end of a one-sided romance. Whether awakening from the dream of love had special significance for Lizzie will never be known. However, it is well known that Lizzie and Andrew shared a close private bond of love, symbolized by the ring of Lizzie's which Andrew wore. If Andrew had shattered that dream of love by any overt or implied act of "discourtesy," it cost him and his complacent (at the very least) wife, Abby, their lives.

Shortly after the trial, Lizzie and Emma moved from Second Street to a large 14-room house on The Hill. They named it Maplecroft. Lizzie changed her name to Lizbeth. Just as there was confusion over the dress she wore, whether plain light blue or fancy dark blue, so there was a fundamental dichotomy to Lizzie's character. One side of Lizzie was in the barn ready to go fishing while her dark side splattered familial blood in her parents' house.

This dual personality began to assert itself in the long, empty years after the trial. No longer the darling of the "Bloomer Girls," (to quote Sullivan), Lizzie found herself also ostracized by Fall River society. She began to cultivate friends in the theater. The most notorious was her liaison with Nance O'Neil, a popular actress of the time. Lizzie the Sunday School teacher (whose hitherto blameless life had helped considerably to win her acquittal) began to throw wild week-long parties for her new theater friends, much to the disgust of the members of the Women's Christian Temperance Union, including Emma Borden. Emma left

Nance O'Neil

after one such episode in 1904 and the two sisters never saw each other again (Sullivan, 208). In 1927, Lizzie died at her home. Emma died at her home nine days later. The secret of that day 34 years earlier went to their graves with them. However, this much is known.

Whether Lizzie Borden was an innocent victim in the Fall River tragedy or the all-American girl with a simple taste for mayhem, her extraordinary words and actions from that bloody day of August 4, 1892, catapulted her family from the narrow confines of their New England lives into the spaciousness of American legend.

■ ■ ■

BIBLIOGRAPHY

"Arrests To Be Made: The Inquiries by Lizzie Borden About Poison Seem Peculiar." *New York Times,* Saturday, August 6, 1892: 1.

"Butchered in Their Home." *New York Times,* Friday, August 5, 1892: 1, 2.

Brown, Arnold R. *Lizzie Borden: The Legend, the Truth, the Final Chapter.* New York: Dell Publishing, 1992.

"Fall River Mystery." *New York Times,* Sunday, August 7, 1892: 1, 3.

Freud, Sigmund. *The Basic Writings of Sigmund Freud.* Ed. Dr. A.A. Brill. New York: Modern Library, 1938.

Gates, David. "A New Whack at the Borden Case." *Newsweek,* June 4, 1984: 12.

Gutheil, Dr. Emil A. *The Handbook of Dream Analysis.* New York: Liveright, 1951.

Hunter, Evan. *Lizzie.* New York: Arbor House, 1984.

Lincoln, Victoria. *A Private Disgrace: Lizzie Borden by Daylight.* New York: G.P. Putnam's Sons, 1967.

"Miss Borden Arrested: Charged With Murdering Her Father and His Wife." *New York Times,* Sunday, August 12, 1892: 2.

Nash, Jay Robert. *Encyclopedia of World Crime,* Volumes I and II. Wilmett, Illinois: Crime Books, Inc., 1990.

Pearson, Edmund, "The Borden Case," Unsolved: Classic True Murder Cases. Ed. Richard Glyn Jones. New York: Peter Bedrick Books, 1987.

Radin, Edward. *Lizzie Borden: The Untold Story.* New York: Simon & Schuster, 1961.

Reach, James. "The Myth of Lizzie Borden," *The Quality of Murder.* Ed. Anthony Boucher. New York: E.P. Dutton & Company, Inc., 1962.

Sifakis, Carl. "Bordenmania," *The Encyclopedia of American Crime.* New York: Facts on File, 1982.

Stuart, Anne. "Lizzie Borden Murder Centennial Marked: Scientist Claims He Found Evidence Missing After Trial." *Santa Cruz Sentinel,* Wednesday, August 5, 1992: A-8.

Sullivan, Robert. *Goodbye Lizzie Borden.* Battleboro, Vermont: The Stephen Greene Press, 1974.